The Benevolence Tax = All Inclusive

UNDEFEATABLE AND ABSOLUTE

by

O. E. Gatson

The contents of this work, including, but not limited to, the accuracy of events, people, and places depicted; opinions expressed; permission to use previously published materials included; and any advice given or actions advocated are solely the responsibility of the author, who assumes all liability for said work and indemnifies the publisher against any claims stemming from publication of the work.

All Rights Reserved
Copyright © 2019 by O. E. Gatson

No part of this book may be reproduced or transmitted, downloaded, distributed, reverse engineered, or stored in or introduced into any information storage and retrieval system, in any form or by any means, including photocopying and recording, whether electronic or mechanical, now known or hereinafter invented without permission in writing from the publisher.

Dorrance Publishing Co
585 Alpha Drive
Suite 103
Pittsburgh, PA 15238
Visit our website at *www.dorrancebookstore.com*

ISBN: 978-1-4809-9616-8
eISBN: 978-1-4809-9596-3

Acknowledgments

A special thank you to President David Zeolla and his staff at Dorrance Publishing Company, who made this book possible.

I Would also like to thank my best friend, J. C. Puryear for his contribution and support on the Job Creation and U.S. Allies Debt Consolidation sections of the book.

Section One

Introduction

Long before the government had implemented a tax system here in America, there was a taxational system in the "Old Country." The raising of taxes has always been an unpopular idea. Little did the Pilgrims know upon their arrival at Plymouth Rock that they would also create a similar tax system. As long as human beings shall live, there will always be a new tax on the horizon. The "Christians" can tell you that long before Jesus had walked this earth there were taxes. We, the people, need an increase in revenue to substantiate the needs of this country, as well as its citizens. Since the United States is simultaneously evolving and progressing toward an unknown future, it is critical that this country be prepared. There will always be the expansion of the infrastructure, healthcare, jobs, and death. Here in America we have a well-structured tax system that has held this country together. As citizens of this country, we must willingly support the emerging of a new tax. This taxation makes our survival in this country more livable and pleasant. However, in acknowledgement of the greatness of the United States, we have missed the recognition of the whole citizen, such as life and death. The focus is now on healthcare to maintain one's life, while refusing to acknowledge that life is only one-half of a person. Our government must make a provision in the tax system for the citizen's death as well. The death of a person must be embraced equally as well as his life, by placing the main focus on the healthcare system. This government may be missing an important component.

Not all persons fly, dance, or go fishing. However, all people will die. Therefore, death should receive the same attention from the government as life. In fact, a death tax should have been one of the first tax laws implemented. Life, whether long or short, is always followed by death. Therefore, death is undefeatable and must become part of the tax system. It is now time to introduce and implement the Benevolence Tax to the American citizens. The Benevolence Tax is a tax to which all workers must contribute in order to maintain an endless source of revenue for the additional upkeep of America.

The origin of the Benevolence Tax had originated during a visit with an elderly person. As the narrative begins, it was a beautiful Spring morning in May. The sun was shining brightly, the birds were singing, and the wind was calm. There was not a cloud in the sky. I thought, *What a wonderful day!* as I was going downstairs to the first floor. I noticed that the house was filled with sadness. Mr. Sam was sitting on the front porch with his head down. Essie was crying because her daddy was dying. Mrs. Applewhite was reading the morning paper. "Good morning," I said to Mrs. Applewhite. She did not respond to me. "What are you reading in the newspaper?" I said to her. She replied, "Bad news." "Oh," I said, "what kind of bad news are you talking about?" I asked her. She said, "A seventeen-year-old boy was murdered last night. The bag lady is missing, and the government is threatening to get rid of the Obamacare." "Why is the government trying to get rid of Obamacare?" I asked her. "I do not know," she said.

Mind you, Mrs. Applewhite is my landlady. Seemingly, she knows everything about the planet. For instance, how many times the dog barks at night, when the groundhog is not going to see its shadow, and who is now sleeping with the preacher's wife. "All right," I said to her. "Let's talk about Obamacare." "No," she said. "I am sick to death of talking about living in this hateful world." "Okay," I said to her, "so, now are you ready to die?" "Well, no, I am not ready to leave this old world just yet. I have a few more good years to live," she murmured. I turned and walked away.

Later that morning, I decided to return to Mrs. Applewhite's room to cheer things up. I lightly tapped on her bedroom door. "Come in," she said. I slowly opened the bedroom door. I walked into the room and sat down. "What is on your mind, my dear?" she asked me. I replied, "Good news!" I told to her the story about my family, friends, and death. I shared with her what it was like not to have had healthcare or a life insurance policy. I told her that it was time for a change in this country. Thus I had finished sharing with Mrs. Applewhite the sad stories. She and I made a decision to look at the brighter side of life. Seeking a way to make our lives better. This would be an effort to aid all humanity. We discussed jobs, healthcare, death, and our great country. Mrs. Applewhite asked me, "What can this president do to help bring a sense of ease to the U.S.?" Without thinking, I said to her, "Can you name the one thing that everyone has in common?" She said, "Well, they have to eat and sleep." I said, "No." She then asked, "What is it everyone has in common?" I said, "The one entity is dying." She and I started laughing. We had laughed about the taxing of death all that day. *What a crazy joke!* I thought to myself at bedtime, as I fell asleep that night.

I awoke before dawn the following morning. I was excited about the promises that I had made to Mrs. Applewhite. I thought it would not be a bad idea to put a tax on death. As I was lying in bed staring at the window, I began to reflect upon the past and my childhood. I remembered a story that my Grandmother Sallie had shared with me when I was six years old. My grandmother was well respected as well as liked in a little town in the South. She was known for being able to pick over three hundred pounds of cotton per day. She had married my grandfather, for he was only good at making moonshine. My grandparents had lived on a huge farm as sharecroppers. Mr. Martin, the landlord, was very good to them, as the story has been told to me. For the landlord would allow them to keep the mule and wagon. They were happy and had decided to have children, of whom their first child was a boy. Two years later, my grandmother said that a cat had jumped over the broom and put her in the family way. Yet to this day, I have been trying to explain to myself how the cat had gotten my grandmother pregnant by jumping over the broom.

It was in the fall of 1926 when Uncle Smokey came by the farmhouse to ask permission to carry my daddy and his little sister to a neighbor's house for a Halloween party. My grandmother had told me that they had just finished eating supper when Uncle Smokey knocked at the door. Jasper, my daddy, was eight years old at the time, and his little sister Griddy was five. Now since my grandmother had named my daddy, it was my granddaddy's time to pick a name for the baby. My granddaddy could not read and write; he had to mark three Xs on sheets of paper and take the paper down to the hog pen. He had left the papers for three days. After the third day, he returned to the hog pen. He had selected the piece of paper that the hogs had not trampled upon. He then returned to the house and named his only daughter Griddy.

It was now getting late, and Uncle Smokey was ready to head for the party. My grandmother had told me that as she stood in the door watching and waving goodbye to her husband, children, and Uncle Smokey, they left in a wagon. She did not have any idea that their lives would change forever, for she told me that she was peeling potatoes when her husband and two children had returned that night. She said that Griddy had gone right to bed without saying her prayers or goodnight. Early the next morning, when she had gone into the bedroom to awaken Griddy, she discovered that Griddy had died. As the story was told, someone had given Griddy a poisoned apple at the Halloween party.

It must have been around midday when Mr. Martin, the landlord, had stopped by to pick up the cotton that had been picked the day before. Being the fine man that the landlord was to them, he took the body and wrapped it in a handmade quilt to take to the undertaker. My grandmother said that for the next eleven years, she had to pay the undertaker one dollar and twenty-five cents on a weekly basis to pay for Griddy's funeral. In reality she was only making four dollars per week. Today, I reminisce about when I used to sit on my grandmother's lap at the age of six. I now realized what she may have been telling me. Sitting here on the front porch, I know that a death tax would have helped her during a very sad period in her life.

Yes, Mrs. Applewhite and I had laughed about the one thing that everyone has in common: death. Now so far I have told this joke to more than five hundred people. No one laughs when I tell the joke about putting a tax on one's demise. They often say, "Putting a tax on death is great." However, there had been one man who thought that raising more taxes on the taxpayer was a bad idea. As a matter of fact, he had told me that I should be ashamed of myself. And only a fool would have thought of such a disgraceful idea about dying. In addition, he told me that it's not a person fault that he or she must die. "Reverend, that is the dumbest idea that I have ever heard. That tax will not pass in Congress." He looked at me and shook his head.

It had been nearly two weeks since I had seen this man. One Saturday evening, someone was at my front door. I had yelled to Mr. Sam to go and see who was at the door, for it was Sugar Daddy at the door (the man who had thought that a tax on death was a bad idea). Well, I could not help thinking what he wanted. As Sugar Daddy entered the kitchen, I noticed he was not smiling. I said to him, "It is so great to see you." He said to me, "Rev., I need to talk to you." I asked, "What is going on?" He told me a long, happy story that ended with a sad twist. He said for over five years his wife and he had been saving for their dream vacation. On the last day of this vacation, they were so happy and ready to take the long trip home, when his wife and he had just received some sad news. As they were packing to return home, Betty, his wife, received a phone call that her Aunt Patty Mae had died. The family had no money and there was not a life insurance policy. His wife was devastated! He proceeded to tell me that there were several disagreements. In addition, the family did not have money to purchase food to feed the guests.

The funeral director was asking for a huge deposit because the family was still indebted for three unpaid funerals. "What must my wife and I do to help her family?" I had appealed to him. "My heart goes out to you and the family." What little money they had was for the return trip home. They would now have to stay at the hotel for another unplanned week. Then, out of the blue, he said to me, "Rev., do you remember that idea about the death tax?" I responded, "Yes." He had gone on to say that it is not a bad idea after all. "Come to think of it, that is the best idea that I have ever heard." "I too," I said. I then took his hand and boldly said, "Let us pray." After we finished praying and embracing, he left with a smile on his face.

Section Two

Methods

Now is the time to find an honorable approach to introducing this tax into society. First we will introduce, define, as well as discuss, the five methods. Contained within the Benevolence Tax are five methods crucial to it perusal, which should facilitate the correct approach to one's comprehension of it. These methods will explain the withholding of the employee's wages, the employer's role and obligation(s), what type of tax, and the refund requirement.

    The employee's Benevolence Tax will understandably be withdrawn (withheld) from his or her wages each pay period. This withdrawal will take place during the entire period of the employee's employment. As an employee, one is given work and then paid for it. What will enhance one's employment is the fact that this tax (Benevolence Tax) does for the employee what no other tax can do, has done, and will do. For the first time in history, the word "tax" will inherit a new meaning. Not only will it take from, but give back, like never before. Let it be known that the taxed will be elated. Now the employee can stop worrying about what is going to happen to his or her family and the unpaid debts that have been left behind. The employee may now feel proud to be an American citizen. Therefore, he or she will be thankful to the government for having the insight to enable a person to die with dignity (new norm). Human beings will rejoice in the fact that whenever, wherever, however their demise may appear, their grief will no longer add to their misery.

The employer will not be obligated to contribute to this fund. Because employers are charged with giving work to others and paying them for their labor, their deeds are often overlooked as to who is responsible for the success or failure among ordinary citizens and/or their families. This tax can lessen the guilt felt after certain hiring practices or the lack thereof. The Benevolence Tax will create a clearer conscience for both employer(s) and employee. The employer may be thankful to the tax system for a well-thought-out plan that has eliminated his or her obligation to contribute to the Benevolence Tax.

Since this is a new tax that has been added to the tax system, this withdrawal will be different from others (i.e., Federal, State, and Local). The term "withdrawal" has, in the past, and even unto the present, meant taking away without the possibility of giving back anything. Any mention of Federal, State, or Local anything has meant discontentment and disgruntlement. With the arrival of the Benevolence Tax, citizens, working or not, can still rejoice knowing that their living, unemployed or otherwise, will give them the ultimate reason for living and a newfound meaning to dying.

The current refund method is wonderful, for it comes at the beginning of a new year. Nevertheless, it is the filing of one's taxes that is costly. With the Benevolence Tax, no refund will be given at year's end. No misunderstanding should come about because of Benevolence Tax. Refunds, even the slightest hint of them, are not what the Benevolence Tax guarantees. However, with the advent of the Benevolence Tax, automatic withdrawals with each paycheck assure the individual that his or her demise for any reason is guaranteed, secured locked in, by way of the Benevolence Tax. Now the employee does not worry about the fact of being late or making a payment on time. There are not any cancellation letters, reinstatement fees, and loss of the money that you have already paid.

Only at the employee's time of death will a refund be issued along with a legal death certificate stating, "TO BENEFICIARY ONLY!"

There will always be room for improvements with the Benevolence Tax. A spouse may be able to ask that this tax be withheld for his or her spouse and children. In time the utilities and mortgage companies may apply for same Benevolence Tax. Anything is possible with this Benevolence Tax and our wonderful country.

Section Three

The Twelve Attributes of The Benevolence Tax

The twelve attributes are the driving forces of the Benevolence Tax. An attribute regards a quality as characteristic. Each of the twelve will be discussed as to how each item can change the attitudes that surround the human demise. Most persons view death as a time of sadness. Thus, one's demise should require a new thought. Humanity must accept death along with all other facets of life. One of the ways to grant acceptance is to be financially prepared with assistance from the Benevolence Tax. Each of the twelve attributes in this section will be defined and discussed. They are public approval, debt consolidation, universal, family, ageless, undefeated, expansion, inexpensive, a no-loophole, non-cancelled, full refund, and non-tangible. These twelve attributes in this section will hopefully give comfort at time of a person's death.

A tax of this magnitude has not been introduced into law. Any opinions that have been given at this point in time are the feedback from a survey that was conducted. Some of the questions that were asked by the people: How can I get this tax withdrawal from my paycheck? How long will it be before this becomes a law? Have you spoken to the senator about this tax? Therefore, the Benevolence Tax is being discussed. Several huge corporations have given their support toward this tax idea. For example, "This is great idea," "Please keep us updated on the progress," "Please contact me on this website," and "How can I help at this time?" Therefore, until the Benevolence Tax goes before Congress to be vote on, statistically, no one has yet to demean or devalue the worth of this new tax's potential.

When a person dies without a life insurance policy, many unpaid bills are left unpaid, such as one's car note, pending utility bills, bank loans, unpaid rent, and anything that has been purchased or acquired by credit. Not only does the death affect emotions, it will also affect big business, along with creditors. Without funds, who is going to buy and pay for flowers, food, gravesite, minister's fee, and the back taxes that might be owed to the government? The Benevolence Tax gives the employee the right to ask that a trustee oversees the refund check. To ensure that the debt consolidation will be honored, bills, etc., will take on new meaning once the Benevolence Tax is enforced.

The Benevolence Tax can be a universal tax. From every corner of this planet, where there is life, death abounds. At the moment of one's conception, death is present. Since death does not discriminate, by making an unjust or prejudicial distinction in the treatment of different categories of people, on the grounds of race, gender, or age, neither will this tax apply prejudicial distinctions. This tax follows death. Therefore, the Benevolence Tax is applicable to all taxpayers.

The seasons of the year will change. However, death still reins. The holidays are not affected by death. Therefore, this tax is not affected by the seasons and holidays. If an employee had to work on the Fourth of July, there is not any need to be alarmed about the withdrawal of this tax. The Benevolence Tax is still reinforced because death and this tax do not recognize the seasons and holidays.

Because the Benevolence Tax is universal, everyone alive will and can benefit from this new tax simply because no one will outlive its usefulness.

The precepts of the family tax are governed today by the application of the law in the tax system for today's dependent(s). In the case of the Benevolence family tax, there is no age limit. In other words, the dependent may remain on the tax-deduction plan, well after the age of twenty-four. Therefore, any of one's family members can qualify, including an employee's parents. Each family member, regardless of age, is included in the benefits of the Benevolence Tax.

No timeline in existence can match the flexibility of this tax. The death is forever here to offer benefits to the worker. The Benevolence Tax is ageless, because death is ageless. For as long as a people may live, they will always be facing their demise. The good news teaches people will live longer in the last days. Of course, technology and the medical field will have a greater need to assist and aid in the extended of a longer life. Although it appears that the technophysics may at this time be out of control, extension weather calamities are here to stay. However, soon the people will rejoice and be at peace, once the Benevolence Tax has been assimilated into our culture. The evil forces that are at work in this society will cease. Gradually, there will be less violence, fewer illnesses, and human beings will live longer. The timeline between death and the Benevolence Tax will be timeless.

Nearly everything comes with a meta-message. For example, the small print at the bottom of a page indicates there is a silent message, in songs, and there is also a hidden message in that skin rash on your body. The Benevolence Tax does not come with any meta-messages. No one is denied on account of his income and the number of his family members. An employee is also qualified regardless to his background, and there is no age limit. It makes no difference if an employee is married or single. Health issues will not affect this tax, and all children are qualified. No one can be denied based on national origin, and everyone is included, the rich or poor. One's race or faith background is unimportant. The state that one may live does not matter to this tax. Since everyone benefits from this tax, every individual can be assured of its benefits. The Benevolence Tax is free of all loopholes and exemptions. The Benevolence Tax has no hidden message, and it is the no-loophole tax.

All of the attributes in this tax are important. However, the no-cancellation stands out from the other eleven attributes. The loss of one's job will not affect the money that has already been withdrawn from one's wages. No divorce settlement or child support will have any effect upon this tax. The only time the United States Treasury Department will issue a refund is at the time of an employee's death. This government policy will remain in effect as long as you live. There are no lapses in your benefits or cancellation for the lack of a missing payment.

Therefore, if an employee should become ill or lose his or her job, the tax money is still safe. The worker does not lose the taxes that have been previously deposited or withheld from one's wages. It is understood to be used only at the time of a person's death. Whether job loss or any situation (unexpected or otherwise), the policy remains in force. Monies yet withheld will not be effected. The policy holder will have no cause for alarm (i.e. cancellation).

The Benevolence Tax has been created for one purpose only: to grant financial help at the time of a citizen's death. Everyone has right to die in peace. This tax can bring a sense of relief to an employee. It's a good feeling to know that your family and loved ones do not have to spend what little funds they have to pay for someone else's funeral. One saves all of their lifetime and is never able to save for the time of demise. When the people of this country realize that death is absolute, is it fair to an employee to have worked most of his life, pay taxes for the upkeep of this country, and then to die only to leave his family without funds to take care of your remains? The Benevolence Tax is only for the sole purpose of one's demise. The tax which can be withheld belongs to the worker. This tax will comes from an employee's wages after the government has taken out the required taxes from the worker's wages. There are no meta-messages here. All participants will receive a full refund (i.e. what a person puts in, he or she will get out of it).

As it has been discussed in the previous section on methods, only at the employee's time of death will refund be issued along with a legal death certificate—TO THE BENEFICIARY ONLY!

All materials currently are being taxed (i.e., food, clothing, shelter,), in addition, cars, alcohol, and tobacco, and notwithstanding. Comparatively, death is not material nor a material attribute of it. For this reason alone, death must be taxed in a differently category. Our government needs to realize death occurs only once in a person life. Therefore, a onetime refund is sufficient. It is a great idea that taxing the citizens for material things in order to be able to support this country. Nevertheless, the tangible part is at war with the non-tangible part of the society. When the people of this society recognize, it is the non-tangible forces that are in control of this world. Then, the power over material things will take it rightful position. The good news teaches that the first shall be last and the last shall be first. When death is first and life is second, human beings will be able to live longer.

The force of death has been misunderstood. Death has been known as the enemy of man. It is important for man to know that death is the last enemy of man. Once death is conquered, human beings will live longer. One must respect death by giving to it the highest honor. It is insane to ignore the greatest force in society. Everything that has been done is centered around death. This is the main reason why taxes have been withheld from your wages. The withheld taxes are used to stop the decaying of the infrastructures of the building, bridges, roads, and health. Decaying is the slow method of dying. Human beings must learn to embrace, honor, as well as respect, death. For death is more powerful than life. This is the main reason for wars. By respecting death, life will automatically be respected.

Therefore, putting a Benevolence Tax in the today's tax system may sound unwise. However, it is very unwise not give to this idea some thought. For life and death are one. Death is the more powerful force of life and itself. The death portion of life should contribute in the maintenance of life. Since death is undefeated and life is defeatable, then by all means the stronger force must aid in the support of lesser force. By way of taxing death, there will be an increase in the funds of the tax system to actually support the healthcare system.

To be able to live a long, healthy life is one of the greatest gifts that have been given to human beings. To be able to die with dignity is also one of the greatest gifts that have been given to human beings. However, there is not any need for life to go chasing after death, for death has always been using the natural GPS of time to find you.

Section Four

The Positive and Negative Aspects of the Benevolence Tax

The Benevolence Tax at this time is only an idea. Therefore, no rules and regulations have been established. Upon the signing into a tax law by the United States Congress, then the citizens of this country will be able to have a clearer understanding of how this tax applies and affects them. In this section, only the commonsense approach can be discussed.

It is very important for the people to know who will make the decision, or decides on the amount of Benevolence Tax that may be deducted from the worker's wages per pay period. Will this tax withdrawal be based on an employee's total wages amount before other taxes have been deducted? Will the worker be allowed to volunteer the amount to be deducted from his or her payroll? There is a strong possibility that the government may decide what deductions to apply.

It is crucial that a worker be aware that minor tax can be applied to the Benevolence Tax that was withheld at year's end. For example, a person has accumulated six thousand dollars by the end of the work year. Will the system view this money as nontaxable, or taxable, provided this a new tax that been made into law? Now the government can view this tax as a taxable savings account and be able to attach an additional one-time fee.

Let's focus on the interest aspects of the Benevolence Tax. Undoubtedly, interest must be applied to this withheld tax. Does the interest belong to the government or the taxpayer? For the government will, by all means, make this decision. Should the tax system allow the taxpayer to share a portion of the interest rate? What will be the amount of this percent to be shared by the taxpayer? Will the interest rate be based on Dow Jones or a flat rate? Well, the system should be allowed to keep all of the interest that has accumulated over the span of the worker's work history. The tax system has done a wonderful deed by assisting an employee with provisions to aid the deceased worker's family at the time of a loved one's death. Now the worker can view death with dignity, even during times of sorrow, without leaving the burden of funeral expenses upon his or her family and loved ones. An employee can also feel great about helping his or her country.

How will an early demise affect the worker's Benevolence Tax refund? As of now, there are no guidelines that have been written in regards to this tax. It has been said that whatever an employee puts in the Benevolence Tax system, only that amount may be paid to the worker's beneficiary-only.

Many people can relate to how insurance companies were there to help their family at the time of a loved one's death. The purpose of the Benevolence Tax idea is not to lessen the importance of insurance companies. The idea is to offer other opportunities to the citizens of this country. It is not easy to keep paying a premium after one has lost employment. For some persons, the thought of losing all of the money which has been paid toward their insurance policies is nothing less than horrific. Now one must start over by purchasing another policy. There is the concern over dying, how will the family pay the cost for the funeral, how can I be a burden to my family, the length of my unemployment, and my friends' opinion of me for allowing these situations to occur.

The Benevolence Tax can eliminate those concerns and give much-needed security. How great to be worry free of the costs that come at the time of one's demise. Now, because of the Benevolence Tax, there will not be any concerns about the cancellation of one's policy, even at the risk of job loss. The over-concern of a direct deposit between pay periods will be less of a focal point for me. There may always be outstanding bills pending. Nevertheless, it certainly will not be the one important bill that should be paid. Doubtless, this tax can offer an employee peace of mind. This peace will certainly play a role in crime prevention. There may be less stress and guilt present. Wow! What a difference the Benevolence Tax will make in a person's life!

Some companies are relocating to other countries. How will the Benevolence Tax be effected and implemented? Can this tax assimilate into overseas tax systems? That may depend upon the relationships between the United States and other nations' tax guidelines. Until the Benevolence Tax has been introduced into a worldwide law, it may be wise not to speculate at the current time. However, an employee should be concerned about this issue. All countries are in need of an increase in revenues. Until the United States has established new rules which might be a major concern for the Benevolence Tax, an employee should consider reviewing the company rules and regulations this company has in regards to the benefits of its overseas employees.

Will this tax be voluntary or mandatory? After this tax has been studied by Congress, hopefully its formability will cause the members of Congress to recognize the multiform of the Benevolence Tax. After the formation and format have occurred, only then shall this be formalized. During this time of the formulating of this tax, the decision of volunteer or mandatory can be made. It is highly possible that any thought of this tax will take a premier position. At any rate, the Benevolence Tax will move forward gradually, whether voluntary or mandatory.

On one's speculation alone, common sense tells you that the Benevolence Tax aids the diversities of a system's needs. For example, the Church is structurally diversified, in this place of structure from the minister on down the chain of leadership. This tax may be of great aid by means of finance. The pastor has his or her own personal obligations. In order for the pastor's needs to be met, Church members must pay the pastor a huge salary. The pastor's life has not been inactive. As the pastor travels to different functions on the behalf of Church, allowances must be considered. Who will pay for the pastor's travel expenses? Should Church members be obligated to make provisions for the pastor? Is the pastor paid out of pocket? In most cases, the Church members will feel obligated to pay for these provisions. However, oftentimes the congregation will be asked to pay for pastor's trip.

Still, there is the upkeep of the Church. Members have their own private lives to maintain. There are jobs losses, illness, divorces, deaths, educational costs. These are basic needs that are common in any arena. Each of these factors can put a burden on a church as well as members. Several members have lost their jobs and are out of work. Some members are sick and out of work. There have been several divorces, which means a loss of funds. Death is occurring on a monthly basis, and sometimes weekly. School supplies can be very expensive for back-to-schoolers. Tuition for college is very costly for some students, and affordable childcare has been a hardship on families for years.

Now the Benevolence Tax can certainly be of aid and comfort to the Church as well as church members. If you are unemployed because of job loss, you can now feel at ease and not worry about the lapses of an insurance policy. Because of the Benevolence Tax, one cannot lose, for the already invested money that has been withdrawn is safe in the tax system. Now you do not need to be concerned about how to make ends meet. Because of the Benevolence Tax, the government has more revenue to give assistance to the unemployed. For now this out-of-job worker can feel at ease knowing that everything will be just fine. Now a visit to church can be a rejoicing time of rejoice.

To be out of work because of an illness can be very stressful. The Church also suffers when its members are out for any reason. This absence affects the dues, tithings, and offerings. These funds are needed to support the activities and functions of the Church. However, it is a great feeling to be able to know that everything has been taken care of in terms of the sick person's demise. The Benevolence Tax was withheld years ago; however, the church member can now relax because of the deductions of the Benevolence Tax from his or her wages. This person may now receive the best of care from the healthcare system. The government has more money to invest in healthcare. Now this member of the church can really give thanks for the check that has been sent to the church. Also, this member will be able to face the time of death with a sense of peace, knowing that his debts will be paid. Creditors will be happy that they were also paid. Again, the Benevolence Tax has touched the lives of the people. Everyone benefits from this tax, such as marriages, churches, hospitals, mortgage companies, utility suppliers, funeral homes, car dealerships, criminal justice system, and social services departments.

Marriages are affected by this tax. A spouse can have a very difficult time if a life insurance policy for his family is unaffordable, depending on how many children are in this family. At the time of a death in this unit, there will be many things that need to be considered: money for food, feeding the immediate family, friends, and guests. The purchase of food can costs into the hundreds of dollars, let alone the utensils and a place to serve the guests and family. The cost of the funeral will be in the thousands of dollars. In most cases, clothing is needed, also the housing for the out-of-town visitors and family members. There may be absentees from work. That will cost an additional lack of financial problems. Even the cost of flowers can be very expensive. How will these needs be provided for without the necessary funds available?

Now if there existed a Benevolence Tax that has been included in our present tax system, a married couple could ask that this be withheld from either employee's wages for each family member. That may include the children, as well as the in-laws. Since this tax has not been formulated, there is no legal status to proclaiming the in-laws cannot be included in the Benevolence Tax portion of the tax system, which has yet to become the law of the land.

However, the Benevolence Tax can be of great assistance to a family in the time of a family member's demise. The Benevolence Tax refund check allows a family to feel at ease knowing the bills can be paid. This tax will aid in all final expenses that one may take an extended leave of absence from his job. This tax also allows the family time for benevolence process to take effect. However, this process may take up to twenty-four months. This Benevolence Tax allows the family members to be able to heal and adjust to a life without the absent loved one. This can be a very challenging time for family. A simple task can become a problem. Who will take the dog for a walk now that my husband is no longer here? I need help in cleaning the house, for my wife was the housekeeper in the family. Sometimes I miss my son's hugs and laughter.

The Benevolence Tax benefits everyone during the time of bereavement. Life can be wonderful when one is not burdened with the guilt of shame for not being prepared at time of a spouse's demise. The tax cannot heal a heart that has been broken. However, this tax can relieve the financially burdened and help one through the time of loss.

Section Five

The Benevolence Tax: A Non-Discriminating Tax

The Benevolence Tax is a non-discriminating. It does not matter who you are, just as long as you are breathing. You will pay this tax. No one is exempted from contributing to tax. The qualification for this tax is death. Therefore, if one is receiving aid for dependent children, one must still pay this tax. The Department of Social Services will honor this tax law. For example, if one is receiving six hundred dollars for three children, the Department of Social Services will deduct ten dollars on a monthly basis for each child one has applied for aid. In the case of accident, the funeral has been taken care of. Plus, this will also mean the Department of Social Services has created a new department for this service, thereby creating more jobs for one's city.

It matters not if a person is rich or poor—no exceptions. This will be a new law on the book, which means old laws do not apply. If one qualifies for any government assistance, this tax can be withheld. Any foreigner that is employed in this country must honor this law. Wherever one lives on this planet and is classified as a citizen of this country, he or she must respect and honor this law. Now it may take some time before this can be fully implemented. Nevertheless, at some point, eventually this tax law will go into effect. The

Benevolence Tax is a new-age law. The Constitution guarantees the right to free speech. However, it does not guarantee people the right to die at the expense of someone else's money.

The penal system will be affected by this new tax law. The government has the right to deduct from the overall cost during one's imprisonment. Therefore, the government must create a new department in the penal system to oversee this department. This will means more jobs which have been created by the government. Now one might be wondering, who will be the beneficiary of this deducted fund? Well, after the final expenses have been paid, the remaining fund that was withheld will be kept by the government. Please be mindful of the fact that the withheld funds belong strictly to the citizens of this country. Whatever funds remain, the government may continue to use at its own discretion to maintain this country's progress.

It is unfair to the citizens of this country to continue carrying burden for someone else's needs. We, the people, are tired of paying taxes on things that someone else may enjoy. Therefore, there is only one thing in this world that we all have in common. That one thing is death. For this force of death has been so misunderstood, it should be the one entity that keeps us together, not apart. Persons must be taught the true meaning of death in this society, for death is all around and one cannot escape it. Now is the time to make death our friend, for death is a protector. However, it is now being thought of as a destroyer, for man has wronged death. Each time one prays to God, one will thank God for everything—except death. How do you think death feels? Death is the last enemy of man. Now citizens, in a very positive way. This tax will keep our country great. Therefore, like the Church says, Amen!

The time has come for humanity to take the sting out of death. After death has lost the sting, man will be able to honor, embrace, and respect death. Only then will death stop allowing itself to be used as a weapon to take a life. Though people may live a longer life, the Benevolence Tax is the first step toward accepting death.

Section Six

Young People

Now I am going downstairs to share with Mrs. Applewhite what I have been reading about the Benevolence Tax. Hopefully, she will approve of what I have to say to her about this tax.

I begin by saying the time has now arrived for a new tax. This tax will be aimed at young people who are entering the workforce. The present tax system is great. However, this country is steadily moving forward. Along the way it must adopt new ideas, for the youth will be bringing into society fresh ways of doing things. This does not mean that the present ways of doing thing change. It does mean that there is always room for growth and progress. Young people have a right to help shape their future. This tax can mean fewer worries; for example, car insurance may be less expensive, but why pay more for an accidental death premium when the Benevolence Tax covers one's demise? Again, job creation will be needed. Therefore, insurance companies are in a position to start a unit to oversee this entity.

As a matter of fact, this tax can be helpful to the insurance company, until an employee has accumulated enough Benevolence Tax in the system to cover the total cost for his or her final expenses. The insurance company may work with the tax system to offer their ideas to fill in the gaps. Nevertheless, a cancellation must not be an option. A worker has every right to ask that a specific insurance company be his or her beneficiary. The beneficiary (insurance company) may take on a new role by eliminating the delay process. It now acts as trustee can issue the refund check and be reimbursed by the system, and therefore more jobs would be created in the process.

It is not the purpose of this tax to hurt the insurance companies, for they have always known that death should be incorporated in the makeup of our government. Therefore, the people of this country should be indebted to these companies and render to them their highest respect for the pioneer role in recognizing the need for death assistance. Now the government is in a position to have the overdue resources in aiding the growth and continual development of this great nation. The Benevolence Tax may play a small role in this endeavor. Nevertheless, the reward is great, without a doubt.

Section Seven

Senior Citizens

Well, Mrs. Applewhite has not interrupted me at all. I had thought to myself that maybe she was waiting for me to talk about how this Benevolence Tax affects the senior citizens of this country. Now, the last thing this new tax needs is for senior citizens feeling overlooked and left out of the scheme of things. So I continued by acknowledging the great job that the elderly have done for this nation. Then I immediately feared this would take the rest of my day. So I started again by saying this to Mrs. Applewhite. "This is what the Benevolence Tax is all about: This tax is about securing provisions for the seniors, for an employee will not always be youthful. This tax would not serve its purpose if it is strictly solely for young people. That means that one must die at a young age. This tax is about an objective and relative to a newcomer entering the workforce."

This tax's purpose is to help the worker feel good about himself. Only then is he as an employee able to do well on the job. Now as the years go by, one day you will realize this in terms of age. For you may be young at heart, but not in age. Now, because of this tax, you will have peace of mind knowing at the time of your demise you will not leave your family and loved ones with the burden of funeral expenses. Who knows how the Benevolence Tax modification in the future will be? There must be room for growth, even with this tax, for it is a known fact that anything that is successful never stands still.

Imagine twenty years hence, the Benevolence Tax has been implemented. There can be other facts to consider. For example, an employee had started working at the age of seventeen. This worker is now sixty-three years of age. This person has invested in this tax to the government for a total of forty-six years. There may be a new program that yet was created solely for this purpose. A foreclosure may be deducted from this system to save your home. However, the funeral cost must be a factor in this decision, such as, how much revenue have you accumulated in the Benevolence Tax's account that you have loaned the government? For example, there is fifty-one thousand dollars. You are in arrears for the amount for the sum total of thirty-three hundred dollars. The cost of a funeral is twenty-five thousand dollars. A retired worker still has in the sum of twenty-two thousand, nine hundred dollars in the Benevolence Tax system. Of course, there would be a stiff penalty involved to deter this transaction from reoccurring.

Since this tax is not yet a current law, one would only be speculating about its future outcome. Hopefully, a prudent mind will recognize the need for such a new tax. Until that time arrives, it is a great feeling knowing this country will not fail the people.

Section Eight

No Living Relatives

While I had stepped from the sitting room to accept a telephone call, in the sitting area I noticed, upon my return, that Mrs. Applewhite had written some notes on a pad. By the look of her non-verbals, I decided to continue unless she asked me to stop for a moment. Now a moment to Mrs. Applewhite could very well mean two hours. I was ready to talk about what could happen if an employee had no living relatives. What would happen to the Benevolence Tax refund check which was scheduled to be paid to a beneficiary at the time of the demise of an employee?

Since there are no rules in regards to this tax, I had thought maybe the worker would be allowed to give this refund to a favorite charity. Of course, why not ask that the refund check be offered to the person that would be responsible for the handling of the funeral? In all fairness, why not allow the government to keep the refund tax money? To continual to supporting our schools, the Social Services Department, Law Enforcement, and healthcare, etc., the military can always use the funds to keep this country safe.

Again, the Benevolence Tax is a tax which can give aid to every entity on the planet. Why not include one's pets, at the time of a person's death? Who would be responsible for the care of the dog or cat that no longer has its owner to provide for the care the animal needs? There is the upgrade for Department of Transportation that can use the funds to help maintain the roads during the inclement weather. Let's not forget the firefighters who risk their lives along with policemen, postal services, and the libraries. As one can see, the Benevolence Tax has the potential to give aid to everything on this planet.

Besides, the government already has taxes to support the needs of this country. This tax will give to this nation the extra funds to ensure that every student in this country would have an opportunity to get a college education without the burden of student loans, which may take years to repay. Once again, the Benevolence Tax may help provide the long-needed extra revenue. Thus, it has been said the primary goal of this tax is to give assistance to the worker's family and loved ones at his or her demise. Nevertheless, the Benevolence Tax will one day become a tax law in this country. Our young people will implement it, as well as assimilate this tax into law. Young people are the future of this country—tomorrow world, in which they are the political leaders.

Section Nine

The Criminal Justice System and the Benevolence Tax

When society starts to focus on the criminal justice system to make necessary changes, it should begin at the point of the self-worth of an individual. If a person feels good about himself or herself, only then can the necessary changes come about. To feel good about one's self starts at the time of conception. It may by safe to recognize the fact that the self-worth of a person started over thousands of years ago. The self-worth of a person is a generational after-fact of character. More than likely, if the foundation of a soul lacks self-worth, this lack of self-worth will then manifest itself to the natural realm from the unnatural realm. At the time of birth, everyone only sees a beautiful baby. Nevertheless, the lack of self-worth of the soul is still present.

This soul in the human body is developing right along with love, hate, go, stop, wet, dry, and everything else in this world that has been known to people. In time this person may do wonderful things in life. He can drive a bus, become a teacher, study to become doctor, or minister, etc., yet the lack of self-worthiness may be still in dormancy. However, there is a cure for the lack of self-worth. This healing starts with just one moment in time. Yes, the truth is it only takes one moment in time to heal the lack of self-worth in a person's life.

The Benevolence Tax can play a vital role in this transformation. The very moment an employee learns that this tax has been withheld from his or her wages, the worker will be conditioned to adopt a new attitude, for this represents something that is personal. The other taxes that have been withheld represented an impersonal withdrawal. The personal tax allows a person to feel that it's all about him or her, such as the feelings of warmth, appreciation, respect, its acceptance, nurturing, and value. Now an individual may view the criminal justice system from a different perspective. To avoid the committing of a crime, the person may think what a wonderful feeling to be in a position to help his family and country; therefore, the lock-up is not for him.

However, an employee who pays impersonal taxes suffers from the lack of self-worth. He may feel that every time he turns around someone is asking for his money. What do I care about healthcare? I am not sick. Do not mention the police to me. All that they do is ride around looking for trouble. The list continues…. The criminal justice system lacks the amount of funds to be able to sometimes help this person experience that one moment in time. The Benevolence Tax can provide that one moment for the worker who lacks self-worth. It helps the family in time of sorrow and assists the government with an endless source of revenue to support this wonderful country.

Section Ten

The Benevolence Tax and the Rights of U. S. Government

Oftentimes the author of this work has clearly stated that the Benevolence Tax is only an idea that may, in the near future, become a taxable law. Therefore, until this tax has become law, one can only speculate as to the role of the government in regards to this tax. It is time for a new-age tax. A new-age tax can be a tax which begins with young persons who are entering the workforce. It will be left solely to the government to enact the actual age requirement. An age limit will certainly be an entity in which the tax system will address. However, at this time there are many questions that have been asked about the Benevolence Tax.

Some of the questions that have been asked are: Will this tax affect my social security benefits? Will this tax become a law in my state? Does this tax affect my student work-study check? How does this tax affect my military benefits? It is safe to say at this time there are no laws pertaining to anyone's rights.

Hopefully, the citizens' questions can be answered in the near future, until Congress reviews this tax and reaches a decision. Until that time, one must realize that our government has always put the needs of the citizens and this country first.

Section Eleven

The Benevolence Tax and the Military

It has been said that the United States Department of Defense is the best in the world. In order to maintain this great title, the government has to continue to find additional funds. The Benevolence Tax can certainly be a source of revenue to help keep this country safe. One may think that to discuss the four branches of service is to speak in a positive manner. However, the citizens of this country must address the welfare of our veterans. By recognizing the truth, these four branches of services should be the first on the list to receive aid from this Benevolence Tax. No one deserves the best of care from the healthcare system than the veterans.

On Memorial Day, this veteran was on the telephone most of the day trying to find someone to take him to a scheduled doctor's appointment. Now, this gentleman is legally blind and cannot see. To make the matter worse, he takes fifteen different medications daily. He needs a walking cane to be able to support him while he walks. He is an alcoholic and his living arrangement is a disgrace to this country. As the story has been told, the police were called to come to his home because he was disturbing the peace. To make a long story short, he was beaten by a police officer, arrested, and later released on the same day.

This veteran has a right to be angry as well as frustrated. On the day of the appointment, he arrived at the VA Hospital at six-twenty that morning. For on this particular day, patients were to be seen in the order of a first-come basis. However, the unit did not open until eight o'clock that morning. This person represents a wounded Vietnam veteran.

The Benevolence Tax will be an endless source of revenue that the government may be able to use to help maintain better treatment for the veterans of this country. This could have made provisions for this veteran to be able to eat breakfast. Since he had been misled by the system, the person who had taken this veteran to his appointment was unwilling to wait and give him a ride home. The patient, meanwhile, became stressed because he needed to find a way to get home. He was told later by the doctor that the clinic would find him a ride home. The doctor also had told him that the services for which he came to be treated that morning he did not qualify.

This may be one of the reasons the person becomes frustrated and acts out. Again, the Benevolence Tax could have offered the well-needed funds to assist this person in order to be able to receive the complete necessary medical attention which was needed. However, the government should not be held solely responsible, for it is sad to admit that our veterans are not the only citizens of this country who may not receive the quality care in which they not only deserve but have earned. The time has arrived for an endless flow of taxes to help support the needs of all citizens. The Benevolence Tax will do just that, by way of employees' rights to have the Benevolence Tax withheld from his or her wages. In the end, everyone wins, including this country.

Section Twelve

Nature and the Costly of Rebuilding Effective

Oh, yes, the Benevolence Tax may sound wonderful! Nevertheless, how will the government know when it is time to ask the taxpayers for taxes? Why should the people of this country continue to pay taxes? Who has told the people of this country that we need to pay more taxes? Well, Mother Nature is telling man that it is time to create a new tax. She does not think that this world has been listening to her warnings. For if people cannot sustain and provide the ordinary basic needs, how will this world be able to continue to make provision for its people? When calamities are all around, as disasters and more floods, fire, storms, and earthquakes abound, there seems to be a war between man and nature. The more one builds, the more frequent nature will tear down.

    When the crops are destroyed, people can replant. When a car becomes outdated, a person goes to purchase another. After a relationship becomes familiar, persons become involved in another one. When a home burns down, a new house is built, etc. However, when the forces of nature abound, man does not ask for more floods and earthquakes. Why not apply the same concepts to the upkeep of this country? There is a simple method to maintain a steady flow of funds to aid the rebuilding of the loss of basic human needs. It has been made clear by the voice of nature that it is time for a tax, not a tax which comes from material entities, for it has been a known fact that all things of material substance shall dissipate. Even human flesh will pass away. Now people must find something that is not material to tax. There is only one force in all existence that man cannot stop. The very best healthcare system cannot stop it. Persons can put an end to life. Nevertheless, they have not been able to stop death. Therefore, nature is trying to tell human beings that the time has come to embrace and celebrate death, as well as celebrate death with respect. This does not mean that everyone needs to throw a party or pick up a weapon and kill. This simply means that death has now become the last enemy of the human race.

In celebrating, people need to recognize what a positive change can do to help man. Death has always unknowing supported people. Death is big business! It has always supported our healthcare system. Does not the person goes to the doctor, or try to eat a well-balanced meal? Does the media say, "If it bleeds, it leads"? When death has been put in its proper place, it will be not only respected but will become a vital source of revenue. Human beings will not be so eager to kill, and pets will be better taken care of. Everything on this earth serves a divine purpose. What is so harmful or shameful about allowing death to continue supporting this country? One should stop, take a look at a funeral procession, and think about the money that has been just spent.

There is an old saying that opposites attract. For as long as death is looked upon as the forbidden fruit, it will always be used as a means of control. When persons want to demonstrate power, they turn to death. What is the purpose for wars? Would it not make more sense to find a way to give a hug instead of a bullet? This is what the Benevolence Tax will be about. Nature has spoken and this shall give an endless source to the tax system, for a person's demise is absolute.

Section Thirteen

Job Creation

Mrs. Applewhite is still taking notes! Therefore, I must be taking this informal presentation in the right direction. One never knows what goes on in that mind of Mrs. Applewhite. She is probably writing notes about the pastor of her church not having done his job. Since I had mentioned, when Benevolence Tax is implemented, new jobs will be created for the economy. She may be thinking that the church should create a new position by firing the pastor. Well, thank goodness for board members and committees! Now, getting back to the creating jobs. The government will need to form a committee to oversee the Benevolence Tax. This will mean the creation of more jobs.

Jobs will needed to be created on the local, state, as well as the federal, level. There must be job training to teach the different department leaders how to manage the new tax revenue. Such questions will need to be answered. Will an employee need to pay a fee or tax on the withheld Benevolence Tax? This is a form of banking, and maintaining this tax will cause government to hire workers to oversee this tax. Therefore, this will create jobs and training in the areas of accounting, teaching, insurance, law, social services and government, etc. For example, the Social Security Department must hire and maintain a worker to process this increase in funds that a retiree receives if he or she is the beneficiary. Will the retiree be forced to pay a one-time tax fee, since this will be an included tax in the tax system? There are not any rules that have been formulated, for all of the taxes in the system are mandatory. Have you ever heard of a voluntary taxpayer? This is the reason why job creation must be mandatory by the government.

The government needs to realize the workforce is how it (the government) survives. This is a fundamental fact! Without the creation of jobs, how can this country maintain itself? This is why the Benevolence Tax is so important. It is a tax that has been based on an indisputable force. It is a fact of life that human beings must die. Therefore, the Benevolence Tax has positioned itself to be an endless source of revenue for this entire planet, nevertheless, the United States. Notwithstanding this tax gives the actual benefit which will cause people to allow death to take a new meaning. Enter death with honor, or dying with dignity. The working-class citizens would now gladly contribute to a tax which would relieve the awesome burden of having to oversee the death of a loved one, for there will be less stress and anger. Man will live longer and continue to pay more taxes, thereby aiding this great country.

As stated earlier, for this tax to be implemented a new department must be created, along with personnel to oversee its continuance. Because of the very nature of this tax and the interest(s) it will bring, there will be the need for the formation of a department to further carry out its necessity and accomplish its much-needed usefulness. All of its objectives only serve to further its longevity and give its benefactors peace of mind.

For the implementation to be further overseen, each state is duty-bound to maintain this tax. Clear-sightedness must prevail during the implementation of the Benevolence Tax, and long after its initial public introduction, motivation of one's need to be free from the worries and hazards involving death will also give the United States new meaning as never before and never again.

Section Fourteen

U. S. Allies Debt Consolidation

It is true that many of the U.S. allies are facing some of the challenges—the lack of money to make provisions for their country and citizens as well. For once, every country has an opportunity to address this one common issue. Where can the country find more revenue for its citizens? All people are tired of being forced to pay more taxes, and their problems are never solved. There will always be a need for revenue to repair or rebuild the infrastructures, more schools, and better healthcare, etc. There is always the need for jobs. How can America assist these allies facing the same concerns?

    America can help the allies by introducing the Benevolence Tax as a bargaining chip. There are times when war may not be an answer. The U. S. can share the idea of a monetary system which represents institutionally a way of exchanging money provided through a country's economy system. Money will be created by using a debt-based system. No creation of new money, but simply the changing of hands. Modern monetary systems usually consist of the National Treasury, the Mint, and central banks, as well as commercial ones. Therefore, businesses and others enjoined would help to make the Benevolence Tax not only workable but a viable force to be dealt with. When implemented, all workers would become automatically qualified to reap the benefits of the new Benevolence Tax. All allies, upon implementing the tax, would hail its importance and push this importance to their allies as well.

Now, the U. S. has been placed in a position of strength without threatening to use war as a force of power. Of course, the president of this country will not be expected to simply give this idea away to the allies without receiving some benefits for America. This tax may be used in terms of debt consolidation. However, what makes this tax so unique is the fact that it has been based upon an undefeated force. There is not anyone at this time able to say otherwise. The sole basis for this tax is death, for there is no escaping death. As matter of fact, death is big business. What does one think healthcare is all about? Death has kept the insurance companies in business for years. It has been supporting colleges for years. The coroners will tell you that his or her education was not free. The morticians may tell you that it is death that keeps them in business. What about the warnings: "Do not drink and drive"? What about a flood? Is one afraid of being overly washed and cleaned? Or is one afraid of drowning? The list goes on!

The allies want and desire the same way of life as that the Americans want from life. The Benevolence Tax will offer this comfort at the time of a loved one's death. Besides, it will help every nation on this earth to be able to have an endless flow of revenue to support its economy. It has been stated in this book many times, as it is about to be repeated for the last time: Death is absolute.

As for the people of America, the idea of division and separation must be dealt with in order to give the Benevolence Tax its room to operate. The time has arrived for all clear-sighted minds to make room for the one entity of life that affects every living human being: death. In truth, all U.S. allies will, at some time, be affected by this tax and sooner or later will take an adoptive stance.

All living things at one time or another will cease to exist. Once this aspect of truth is adopted, then mankind (allies included) will become one step closer to actuality. The insurance companies, morticians included, have always recognized this inevitable truth.

Monetary systems around the world, whether different or similar, carry the same burden: there is very rarely enough money to properly provide for it citizens. Add to that the fact that jobs often become scarce when the general populace increases beyond its ability to aid and assists as needed. Enter death, and added difficulty abounds, once cooperation becomes ease. Therefore, buying and selling this idea, Benevolence Tax would further bring about the needed proximity. Also, the Benevolence Tax will bring closure to one of the world's most complex, yet simple, facts of life: death. All factors, varied and otherwise, would serve to bring about the enhancement and promotion of the Benevolence Tax. U. S. allies are welcome to the new way of doing business. Everyone wins.)

Section Fifteen

Everyone Benefits from the Benevolence Tax

Any tax which is attached to death is undefeatable, for death is the last thing that will be left standing. Since the beginning of time, people have always had a trade system. The cattle, stones, and land were used in exchange for business. In today's society, money is the major entity that is used for bargaining. Any tax that has been connected to material things will cease at some point. Taxes on homes, cars, and food are not guaranteed. The house might be destroyed by fire. The car becomes out of style and junked. The food has been eaten. That is the end of paying taxes on the home, car, and food, since death is endless and universal. A tax which has been placed on dying will be reinforced no matter where one may live. No tax in existence can match the flexibility of this tax—death is undefeatable!

    The very flexibility of this tax provides even revenue to aid in the construction of various projects (i.e. bridges, roads, etc.) because the government will apply the interest to supply much-needed funds for various endeavors (college education, etc.). Often, the politicians have spoken about the poor condition of the infrastructure of our cities. There are thousands of bridges that are in need of repair. The roadways and just the maintenance of the inner cities alone is very costly. Our government does not have resources, in terms of funds available, to repair, build, and do the much-needed work. Nevertheless, the government continues to find ways to provide funds. At some point, the burden will always be placed on the shoulders of the taxpaying citizens.

The Benevolence Tax is needed, for this will offer the tax system endless sources of revenue. This tax can be used to acquire money for assisting the nursing homes and help to make healthcare more affordable, along with affordable housing. There can be funds available to help our school systems. This tax will provide funds to keep the military strong. The taxes from the Benevolence Tax can certainly help the farmers who are in need of federal assistance. With this tax the support list is endless. Once this tax has been voted into a law, the search for the funds involving the expansion and upkeep of this country will be one less concern for the taxpayers.

Hopefully, by the implementation of this new tax, some sense of ease can be brought to the citizens of country, for this is inexpensive and requires very little effort to achieve on the employee's behalf. A small amount may be deducted from the worker's salary, and each working person will be able to feel at ease. To know that one will not be leaving his or her loved ones with huge bills at the time one's demise is one of the greatest feelings in a person's life.

Section Sixteen

The Conclusion

The history of all things has a way of repeating itself. Think about how the West was won. The pioneer Daniel Boone had the same issues of today. He, his family, and friends were concerned about hunger, violence, faith, healthcare, and death. There was a need for the control of violence. Did he carry a Bible in his hand? Or was that a gun? Rebecca, his wife, had needed assistance during the birth of their son. Was there not a traveling preacher, and did he not go hunting for food? Is it safe to admit that there was tension between the persons that did not think or look like him? Yes, money was still short.

The basic needs for humanity have always been an unresolved issue. Adam and Eve had needed food, clothing, and healthcare, as the legend has been told through the ages. When will people realize that death has always been an issue for all? When there were only four people on this earth? Did not Cain kill Abel? Even at that time, Abel had to be buried along with Lot and David. Therefore, the demise of the people should not continue to frown on death. What is wiser for a person to tax? Should man put a tax on an apple or death? Apples are seasonal; however, death is not a seasonal facet. There is not one component that stops this entity known as death. There is great medical care in the world; however, doctors who have been trying to save lives must die just as patients do. There will come a time when the government will be forced to put a tax on one's demise. The system must be looked upon as an endless source of revenue that even includes dying. Life insurance policies have focused on death. Morticians, the coroners, the list continues on. Everything that one does is based upon avoiding the obvious. People are thinking about avoiding the obvious. For an example, do not forget to wear a life jacket! Will you please buckle your seatbelt! Do not play with guns, etc.

Hopefully, the Benevolence Tax will be recognized as an honorable way of approaching death, for the people of this country will be graceful to a new way of dealing with death, in addition the creating of jobs, aiding our allies, and now an endless source of revenue to continue keeping this country powerful. All citizens of the United States benefit from this new tax. Now human beings can understand that life and death are a reality. Life can be thought of as the feminine side, and death as its masculine counterpart. However, when these two forces unite as one, life will have more meaning to the living, and death as well. Violence, and all it has to offer, will become miniscule and peace will reign supreme. In addition, the U.S. Treasury Department will have at its disposal an endless supply of revenue. Where once the Benevolence Tax was just a thought or a state of mind, it has now become reality. In truth, the Benevolence Tax is here to stay.

www.ingramcontent.com/pod-product-compliance
Lightning Source LLC
Chambersburg PA
CBHW061519180526
45171CB00001B/251

www.ingramcontent.com/pod-product-compliance
Lightning Source LLC
Chambersburg PA
CBHW061519180526
45171CB00001B/251